GOOD LIFE PRACTICE

A Quick Start Guide to Mindful Self-Regulation

Dave Mochel

GOOD LIFE PRACTICE
Copyright © 2018 by Dave Mochel

ISBN 978-0692162293
Applied Attention Press

Top Five Reasons
<u>Not</u> to Read This Book:

1. There is nothing new here. The principles and practices presented in these pages have been around for a long time – some of them for thousands of years. The purpose of this book is to make these principles and practices accessible and applicable in modern life.

2. I am not enlightened. I am a recovering reactive, anxious, perfectionist who needs these practices as much as anyone. Like any other human being, I lose sight of what is most important in the demands and distractions of daily life, and I benefit from practicing what is in these pages.

3. This is not a feel-good book. One of the realities of life is that it contains discomfort. Ironically, finding acceptance for this allows you to experience greater joy as you discover that you are capable of incredible things even when life feels really hard.

4. It is not a quick fix. The subject of this book is a practice – an approach to life that takes time and effort. If you are looking for a breakthrough, an epiphany, or a one-time transformation that will carry you for the rest of your life, then this book is not for you.

5. You don't need fixing. This is not a self-improvement book. One of the goals of this book is for you to realize that you are already enough as you are. You can discover the authentic confidence that comes from knowing that you have always had what you need to deal with whatever shows up.

So Why Read This Book?

Being human is messy. Many of us look shiny on the outside and feel a bit scrambled on the inside. Sometimes we are lonely in a room full of people. Sometimes we feel dissatisfied even when we have everything we need. Sometimes we try to control situations that are completely beyond our influence. And sometimes we try to escape normal human feelings even though we know they will return.

I often think it would be easier to be a badger. I don't know for sure, but I don't think badgers spend a lot of time worrying about being a badger. I think they follow their urges for survival, make more badgers, and sleep. Maybe they have some social gatherings from time to time – to be honest, I did no research on badger lifestyle before writing this part. While badgers may not live a glamorous life, it seems relatively straightforward.

On the other hand, humans are animals with hopes, dreams, and regrets. We are both blessed and cursed with the knowledge that we are human. We can create art and poetry, we can send people to the moon, and we can take care of strangers who are suffering. But we are also capable of yelling at small children about the importance of kindness, worrying about whether we are enough, and protecting our ideas and opinions as if we were protecting our physical selves.

If you find that being human sometimes feels like a bit much…If you are tired of feeling like CNN on the inside while trying to look like Facebook on the outside… If you would like to find just a bit of grace and clarity… If you would like to be more present, purposeful, positive, and connected when the challenges of daily life arise, then this book was written for you.*

* Whenever "you" appears in this book, it refers to all human beings – including me. Don't take anything in this book personally. We are all neurotic – this is something that I love about our species.

Endorsements for Dave's Work

*You are changing lives – I know you have
changed mine for the better.*
~ Matthew Briger, Owner, Sola Salons

*The retreat you led was one of the most valuable
and important things I have done. You gave us
tools to find our common ground, even when
others may frustrate or challenge us.*
~ Tina Rivera, Teacher, Denver, Colorado

*We are more open, more trusting, and just plain
more effective as a result of working with Dave.*
~ Alliya Rivo, Teacher, New York

*I've used the word "transformational" at least ten
times since the workshop, and had extremely
positive experiences practicing mindful self-
regulation.*
~ Nick Machol, CEO, Machol and Johannes

*The techniques and tools Dave has shared with
me had an immediate and sustainable impact on
my relationships, my business results, and my
general wellbeing.*
~ Dan Greenleaf, President, Home Solutions

Dave is one of the few people who inspire me to be a better person.
~ *Greg H. Kubicek, CEO, Holt Inc.*

Dave has taught me how to respond to my emotions in a profoundly positive and productive way.
~ *Alexx Temena, Designer, Oakland, California*

I have never seen anyone combine science, wisdom, and practical application in such a remarkable way.
~ *Beatrice Alexander, Chicago, Illinois*

Gratitude

*If the only prayer you ever say in
your entire life is thank you,
it will be enough.*
~ Meister Eckhart

To Marnie –
*Thank you for teaching me the value of doing the
next right thing. Also, thank you for reminding me
that I am funnier in person than I am in writing –
and that I could work on that.*

To Keller and Eli –
*Thank you for the constant reminder that we can
all grow as long as we live. I am deeply grateful
for your kindness, humor, inspiration, love, and
support. Thank you for the joy of being your
father.*

To my teachers in all forms –
*Thank you for your courage, compassion, wisdom,
and guidance that continue to make all the
difference in my life.*

Acknowledgments

Life doesn't make any sense without interdependence. We need each other, and the sooner we learn that, the better for us all.
~Erik Erikson

The list of resources and further reading at the end of this book is a testament to the contributions of so many who have shaped my thinking.

Having said that, I do want to specifically montion some of the researchers whose work has been the most influential, including David Eagleman, Richard Ryan, Carol Ryff, Sara Lazar, Todd Kashdan, Ed Diener, Ruth Baer, Richard Davidson, Kristen Neff, Roy Baumeister, Richard Tedeschi, Sonia Lyubomirsky, Michael Posner, Stephen Joseph, Robert Emmons, Barbara Fredrickson, Ed Deci, Brene Brown, Robert Kurzban, and Mark Leary.

I also want to express my deep appreciation to Jon Kabat-Zinn for teaching me about the power of mindfulness, Cheri Huber for deepening my understanding of compassion, Marnie Woehr for consistently demonstrating the importance of doing the next right thing, Sandy Ellis for living as a model of unconditional love and kindness, Alexx Temena for being an invaluable source of constructive feedback, Jay Fields for helping me see the need for self-compassion, Sara Caputo for showing me the value of a plan, and my Mom and Dad for instilling in me a curiosity about how and why human beings do what they do.

Finally, I have to give a shout out to my clients – many of whom have given me permission to share parts of their stories in this book. Their humor, courage, and humanity give me hope for us all.

Contents

It is much simpler to buy books than to read them and easier to read them than to absorb their contents.
~William Osler

The Beginning

*The journey of a thousand miles
begins with a single step*
~ Lao Tzu

In my mid-twenties, I punched a wall hard enough to break several bones. The ache in my hand on rainy days is a great reminder of why I practice.

I learned many things when I was growing up, but how to work effectively with the discomfort and uncertainty that comes with being human was not one of them. I thought that a good life was the result of getting circumstances to be just right – the right career, the right friends, the right vacations, the right amount of approval and admiration from others…

In the absence of the control over the universe that I desired, I thought the answer was to appear like I had it all together. I tried really hard to look happy on the outside even though I was struggling on the inside.

1

My lack of life skills and my increasing anxiety eventually created a perfect storm that I now refer to as a nervous breakthrough.

Breaking my hand helped me realize two things:
        1. Something needed to change
        2. I did not know how or what to change

Fortunately, I found many great teachers. They came in the form of colleagues, students, family members, counselors, researchers, and authors.

For the past three decades, I have been studying scientific research and wisdom related to human development, neuroscience, and wellbeing in an attempt to understand the building blocks of a good life. My goal has been to pull together what I have learned and put it in an accessible form that is applicable in daily life.

As a coach and consultant, I train individuals, teams, and organizations in the practice of mindful self-regulation – the subject of this book. I love what I do, and feel deeply grateful that I have this opportunity.

The purpose of this barebones guide is to help you start practicing. While philosophies, epiphanies, or intentions can be helpful, it has become clear to me that on their own they are not enough to create lasting change.

Consistent practice over time, on the other hand, can create absolutely incredible results. And unsexy as it sounds, it is repeated behavior over time that makes the biggest difference.

To that end, in these pages you will find questions to ask yourself and practices to engage in. Rather than reading through quickly and then putting it back on the shelf with your other self-help books, I encourage you to go through the annoying, boring, and humbling experience of practicing something new.

This book is organized into two parts. *Part One: The Human Condition* puts forth some context for what it is we human beings are all dealing with. *Part Two: Good Life Practices* presents a host of exercises you can incorporate into your life if you choose.

3

The book is small – designed to be carried around. The chapters are brief – designed to give you portions you can digest and put into practice. I tried to write the shortest book I could – if I were a more skilled writer, it might have been shorter. I am sure that you will be left with questions – you will find the answers in your practice.

The reason I harp on the idea of practice is because practice allows you to see what you are really capable of. And I can promise you that you are capable of more than you think – we all are.

Someone in one of my classes once told me that the statement "you are more capable than you think" sounds like " self-help, motivational garbage." Ouch, but fair enough.

To be clear, when I say "you are more capable than you think," I am referencing the fact that you have a human brain that purposely hides things from you that you are capable of.

While this may seem like a cruel trick, it does this to protect you. As far as the survival portion of your brain is concerned, you have lived this long without changing it up, so why start now and take the risk of stepping into the unknown?

Full disclosure – there was a time in my life when I thought that if I practiced really hard, I would get somewhere and be done. I brought my perfectionism to my practice and used it as another opportunity to be dissatisfied. Over time, I came to realize that life is just one continuous opportunity to practice. You can think of your practice as your life or your life as your practice – either one works.

One of the great challenges of being human is that we do not know when our time is up. We might have sixty seconds, sixty days, or sixty years. We just don't know. This uncertainty leaves us with the incredible opportunity to practice, to grow, and to love – right up until the point we die, whenever that is.

It is my sincerest hope that you find something helpful within these pages. I wish you well in your practice of a good life.

PART ONE:
THE HUMAN CONDITION

*Life is like playing a violin solo
in public and learning the
instrument as one goes on.*
~ Samuel Butler

Being Human

People are just people, and all people have faults and shortcomings, but all of us are born with a basic goodness.
~Anne Frank

Have you ever been stuck in traffic? Maybe you found yourself gripping the steering wheel tightly, practicing some new sign language, or crafting stories about the other drivers. Maybe you beat yourself up for not having left earlier or tortured yourself with disaster scenarios resulting from being late. Or…maybe you practiced being grateful you have a car to drive. Maybe you spent your time wishing that the drivers around you would arrive at their destinations safely and have a healthy and happy life. Maybe you marveled at the fact that you have thumbs….

7

Traffic doesn't happen to you. You are the traffic. Has this ever occurred to you? There you are looking around at the other drivers feeling like a victim, and they are looking at you feeling the same way. We are participants in the traffic.

Life isn't happening to us. We are participating in life. How we participate makes a huge difference – for us and for everyone around us. This is how it is being human.

Being human is complicated. We are bombarded by urges and thoughts that are connected to automatic behaviors. Sometimes this leads us to do stuff that does not align with what we really value.

Have you ever yelled at a small child about the importance of kindness? I have. There you are, standing over this little human being while you lecture him in a stern (and maybe loud) voice about how crucial it is that we treat other people with kindness and respect. Despite the conflict between the content and the tone of your message, you feel justified and satisfied – as long as you don't look too closely or too long at the child's face.

8

We can call it hypocrisy or we can call it humanity. All of us have gaps in our lives between our values and our behavior. This is because the human nervous system has a complicated evolutionary history. Our drive for survival can feel like it is in conflict with the values that give life meaning. At some level we are all neurotic, compulsive, irrational and hypocritical. We can develop a sense of humor, honesty, and compassion about this, or we can pretend that we are immune to being human.

Because we are human, we have a great tendency to:

Get distracted and triggered by the events of daily life and lose sight of what matters most

Limit ourselves by becoming attached to circumstances we like and avoiding circumstances we do not like

Exhaust ourselves by resisting life as it is and trying to control circumstances that are outside our control

9

Because we are human, we have a great capacity to:

Work peacefully with whatever shows up in life

Focus powerfully on what is important and what is needed

Practice the relationship to life that we seek

We can learn to work more skillfully with our humanity. We can grow our capacity for a good life with daily practice. A large body of research on human wellbeing points to some skills that are fundamental to a good life. These skills are strengthened with practice.

This practice may seem abstract at first. However, practicing mindful self-regulation is as real and concrete as practicing a tennis serve, a song on the piano, or arithmetic.

This practice may seem awkward at first. This is completely normal. Right now, if you asked me to serve a tennis ball over the net and into the opposite court, it would look a lot like a cat taking a shower – a lot of frantic movement and strange noises. This is not because there is something wrong with me; it is because I have not played much tennis at all. If I continued to practice, there is good reason to believe that I would look and feel less like a desperate caged animal on the court. The same is true for you and the practice of mindful self-regulation.*

The bottom line:

Because we are human, we have areas of our lives where our behavior does not align with our values. We have a profound ability to align our life with our values – it just takes practice.

*This is not to say that you will look or feel like a desperate caged animal when you practice mindful self-regulation – I just needed a metaphor.

Practice

Under duress, we do not rise to our expectations - we fall to the level of our training.
~Bruce Lee

"It is the same every morning. He resists getting up, forgets his socks or his lunch, I yell at him, and he goes to school with both of us feeling crummy." Julie told me this with tears in her eyes. Each morning she would cross her fingers and tell herself that it was going to be different. Then the feelings of frustration would arrive and she would go through the same routine. After all, she had been practicing it for a long time. Rather than continue to hope that tomorrow would be different, she began to practice accepting that the feelings of frustration were going to show up. This allowed her to focus on what she was going to do when they did. She became quite skilled at recognizing the sensations early, feeling her feet on the ground, taking a breath, and bringing to mind how much she loved her son. From this place she was able to hold him accountable and support him without a battle.

We get what we practice. When we are angry, we experience anger. When we are loving, we experience love. This wisdom has been around for a long time. The Law of Karma translates into "We get what we practice." The Golden Rule tells us that when we "Do onto others as you would have them do onto you," you also get the benefit of whatever you are doing.

What do you imagine the world needs more of? Practice that. If you would like more love in your life, then the most direct route is to practice being loving. If you want acceptance, gratitude, kindness, or joy in your life, then the most direct strategy is to practice being accepting, kind, and joyful.

We get better at what we practice. Your brain is constantly rewiring itself to become more skilled at what you do repeatedly. Modern science tells us that your brain is continually building or dismantling connections based on what you do. Skill is a matter of connectivity in your brain. The stronger and faster connections are, the more comfortable and automatic a behavior becomes. This is true for physical, emotional, social, and mental skills. Deliberate, conscious practice is the

13

quickest path to building new connections in your brain.

We are always practicing something. Your brain does not care whether you want to get better at something, it only cares that you do it. When you sleep at night, your brain organizes itself to get better at what you did during the day. This is how a habit is formed. When you argue, you get better at arguing. When you listen, you get better at listening. When you complain, you get better at complaining. When you treat yourself or others harshly, you get better at that. When you treat yourself or others kindly, you get better at that...

New practices can be uncomfortable. Learning a new skill requires practice, and practice requires effort. Your brain likes to save energy, and it connects what you have done in the past with your current survival, therefore it can be resistant to trying new things.

This is where New Year's resolutions go to die. Don't believe me? Try this – clasp your hands together with your fingers interlaced. Now change it up so that your fingers are in a different order. Feel the difference? Try brushing your teeth with the other hand…

There are several ways your brain tries to steer you back to your familiar way of doing things.

It uses discomfort. It creates some discomfort when you do new things or think about doing new things.

It uses rules. It tells you that "you can't," "you shouldn't," or "you aren't that way."

It forgets. It conveniently forgets to put things on your to-do list or your calendar.

When you have a hiccup in a new practice, it uses this as a reason to give up and go back to the old behavior.

Knowledge is not practice. One clever strategy that your brain uses to avoid adopting new practices is to use knowledge as a substitute for practice. For example, knowing that exercise is good for you does not give you the benefits of exercise. However, knowing that exercise is good for you can give you an excuse not to exercise. Knowledge is not practice – practice is practice.

You are practicing something right now.
The awareness and acceptance that you are always practicing something can be incredibly useful. You can catch on to the ways that your brain steers you away from new behavior and back to old behavior – even when that old behavior is not working for you. You can take complete responsibility for whatever you are practicing without judgment or blame.

The bottom line:
Be careful what you practice, because you are going to get better at it.

Ask yourself

What is something that you practice regularly that really works for you?

What is something that you practice regularly that is not really working for you?

A Good Life

*My mission in life is not merely to
survive, but to thrive; and to do so
with some passion, some compassion,
some humor, and some style.*
~ Maya Angelou

Growing up, I worked on a farm in the summer
putting up hay. Temperatures in the barn could
easily reach one hundred and twenty degrees. A
conveyor belt carried heavy bales from a wagon
outside to a hole high in the wall of the barn. The
bales dropped around us and kicked up clouds of
dust and chaff that filled the air, stuck to my
sweaty skin, and seemed to coat my entire throat.
My arms were exhausted and covered with red
scratches from hauling the bales into place. I was
miserable. Steve, a farmhand in his fifties, stacked
the hay at an unimaginably fast pace. Sweating
more than anyone I had ever seen, he never
stopped smiling. I vividly remember a moment
when we were resting and waiting for another
wagon to pull up. Steve looked over at me
grinning and said, "Isn't this great!?"

A good life can contain it all. A good life contains joy, discomfort, loss, triumph, disappointment, surprise, routine, upset, love, anger – the whole deal. Being well is not about suppressing or avoiding some feelings and clinging to others. Bringing awareness and acceptance to whatever shows up allows you to learn from it, and to choose a response that is aligned with your values, goals, relationships and commitments.

This is not new. The concept of the good life has been around for thousands of years – before the Internet, smart phones, and salted caramel dark chocolate. Wisdom from lasting traditions such as Stoicism, Humanism, Buddhism, Judaism, Christianity, Islam, and Hinduism all speaks to the importance of embracing the miracle of existence and working with it, rather than trying to bend it to your will.

The pursuit of happiness leads to more pursuit, not happiness. Many of us were taught – directly or indirectly – that the secret to happiness, satisfaction, and fulfillment is "success" – going to the right school, having the right career, getting the right people around you, and so on. The idea is that if you can get circumstances to be the way they are "supposed" to be, then happiness will follow.

Having the "right stuff" does not remove the fundamental challenges of being human. Having access to more material resources than at any time in human history has not squelched our anxiety, dissatisfaction, stress, depression, or loneliness. In fact, these psychological challenges are on the rise despite our increasing wealth, greater access to conveniences, and the development of incredible technology.

No matter how successful you are, you cannot arrange your life to avoid all discomfort. You cannot get people, emotions, and circumstances to be just the way you like them. The reality of being human is that you have a nervous system that creates a whole range of sensations – some of these are pleasant and some are not.

A good life contains both purpose and pleasure. Having a sense of purpose is just as vital to wellbeing as being able to enjoy pleasant experiences. Growth, meaning, contribution, and learning are fundamental to a good life, and these can be practiced even when life is not comfortable. There is an asymmetry between purpose and pleasure – while connecting with purpose often makes life more pleasurable, focusing on pleasure often makes life less purposeful.

A good life embraces the challenge and the miracle of being human. Life often does not show up in the way we want it to. The choice to embrace this or fight against it has an enormous impact on the quality of our lives. We can learn to live wholeheartedly with the fact that life is both miraculous and challenging.

The bottom line:
A good life often boils down to peaceful and powerful relationship with whatever is happening.

Unconditional Wellbeing

When you arise in the morning, think of what a precious privilege it is to be alive - to breathe, to think, to enjoy, to love.
~ Marcus Aurelius

Maggie was in her forties and had a lot to live for. This is why I was completely caught off guard when she told me that her terminal diagnosis was the best thing that had ever happened to her. She told me that her whole life she had been seeking love by pursuing accomplishment and achievement (and she was quite accomplished). However, each goal she reached was followed by a sense of disappointment when the fulfillment she sought did not follow. Looking down the barrel at something that was completely unwanted and outside her control had led her to a life-changing conclusion. She realized that whatever was happening in her life was an opportunity to practice being loving. Sadness, fear, anger, and frustration were no longer reasons to blame or complain. They were opportunities to be as loving as possible. She told me that she had more love in her life in since the diagnosis than she had had in the previous forty years.

Conditional wellbeing is shaped by what shows up. Events, people, weather – stuff shows up around us because we live in a complex universe. Sensations, emotions, and thoughts – stuff shows up within us because we are human beings with complex nervous systems. We like some of the stuff that shows up, and we do not like other stuff that shows up. We don't really get to choose what shows up in life. This is just how life is.

Unconditional wellbeing is shaped by what we practice. In addition to what shows up, there is where we choose to put our attention and energy. What we practice includes the training we do to build skills or cultivate internal resources. It also includes how we respond to what shows up in the moment. Choosing what we practice is at the heart of unconditional wellbeing.

Circumstances are real. I am definitely not suggesting that having a good attitude or thinking positively will make oppression, poverty, injustice, illness, injury, loss, and discomfort go away. I am suggesting that focusing on what we practice allows us to address these challenges consciously and purposefully, rather than letting them determine the quality of our lives.

The outside-in approach is popular. Many of us work very hard to get circumstances the way we want them, hoping that this will lead to the internal experience we seek. We look for the person who will trigger an internal feeling of love, the beautiful setting that will trigger pleasant feelings of relaxation or awe, or the achievement that will trigger feelings of joy and satisfaction.

A significant part of our wellbeing is unconditional. There is nothing wrong with the outside-in approach, but it is limited by the fact that what shows up is constantly changing. When we focus on what we practice, we can optimize our wellbeing within the inevitable constraints of life. The more we practice working peacefully and powerfully with whatever shows up in life, the less the quality of our lives depends on circumstances that are outside our control.

Happiness is not normal. We are not biologically designed to feel good all the time. The reality is that happiness is one of many healthy human experiences.

24

We live in a society that sees feeling good as the gold standard. Pleasure, preference, comfort, satisfaction of craving – these are great tools for selling products, but not always the best guides for a good life. The cultural infatuation with comfort can leave us with the idea that everything other than happiness is a problem to be avoided or fixed. It can also lead us to compulsively seek comfort and resist discomfort – even when this costs us the life we really want.

You can practice what you seek. Rather than trying to get your circumstances to trigger a feeling, you can cultivate what it is that you want to experience internally – love, acceptance, peace, gratitude, connection, or joy. This is the ultimate shortcut. Whatever it is that you want to have more of in your life – practice that.

This is not about what you should do. This is about what you choose to do with what you can do. You have the ability to practice presence, purpose, cultivation, and connection. You have the ability to strengthen your awareness, acceptance, clarity, compassion, gratitude, and awe. You can pay attention and let go of resistance and clinging. You can love unconditionally, build healthy and supportive relationships, choose action purposefully, and take complete responsibility for your life – no matter what your circumstances.

Your relationship to your thoughts and sensations is key. Each of us has autopilot responses to what shows up in life. Some of these responses are aligned with our goals and values, and some are not. We can build awareness and acceptance of our conditioned responses to life. We can gain clarity about the nature of our thoughts and sensations. Awareness, acceptance, and clarity allow the opportunity for a conscious response to what shows up.

You have the gift of self-regulation. You can choose behavior based on goals and values rather than counting on circumstances and automatic conditioning to determine your behavior. You have the capacity to focus your energy on what is most important to you – even when you don't feel like it. The ability to take purposeful action in the face of conflicting impulses, urges, and habits is a rare ability in the animal kingdom – and you have it! This ability allows you to consciously shape your brain, align your life with what really matters, and support the wellbeing of others.

This is not about self-improvement. This is the development of a lifelong practice to support unconditional wellbeing – for you, for others, and for the world. No matter who you are, there are always new things to discover about yourself and the people around you. You will never run out of opportunities to fall down and get back up again, to discover a limiting belief or an ineffective habit, and to grow wiser as a result. In this process it is normal to get bored, feel resistance, become overwhelmed, or to completely forget to practice altogether. When this happens, you can simply begin again.

The bottom line:
While you cannot choose what shows up in life, you have an incredible capacity to choose what you practice. This choice has a profound impact on the quality of your life.

Ask yourself

If you focused more on what is
under your control, what
difference would that make in
your life?

The Fundamentals

The good life is a process,
not a state of being.
It is a direction, not a destination.
~ Carl Rogers

Mindful self-regulation strengthens four fundamental skills of unconditional wellbeing:

Presence. Being with what is

Purpose: Focusing on what matters

Cultivation: Practicing what you seek

Connection: Being of service

Presence: Being with what is

Presence is the skill of consciously bringing awareness, acceptance, and clarity to what is happening within you and around you.

By increasing awareness, acceptance, and clarity, we can learn to be in the presence of the natural discomfort that comes with being human. Rather than avoid discomfort or failure, we can use it as feedback about our strategies and effort. We can learn to work more peacefully with complex and ever-changing circumstances. Stepping back from the reflexive avoidance or clinging to thoughts and sensations allows space for connecting with purpose.

Purpose: Focusing on what matters

Purpose is the skill of putting your time and energy into what you value and accepting responsibility for the consequences of your choices.

Purpose is the seat of power. Human beings have an absolutely incredible capacity to self-regulate behavior based on what is most important. This is unique in the animal kingdom. Rather than be guided solely by how we are feeling in any given moment, we can choose principled action based on lasting values, goals, commitments, and relationships. Further, a great source of freedom is the acceptance of responsibility for the choices we make and the consequences that follow.

Cultivation: Practicing what you seek

Cultivation is the skill of accessing and cultivating powerful internal resources such as courage, faith, compassion, gratitude and awe

While our brains are already wired based on our genetics, our past environments, and our past behavior, they are continually being rewired based on what we do. This is known as behavior-dependent neuroplasticity, and it means that we do not have to wait for circumstances to trigger the internal experiences we seek. We can access and strengthen positive internal resources. The more we practice this, the more independent of circumstances our wellbeing becomes.

Connection: Being of service

Connection is the skill of seeking to understand, being supportive, and communicating clearly and kindly.

Human beings thrive in community with others – it is fundamental to our wellbeing. By listening, understanding, communicating assertively and compassionately, and reaching out supportively, we improve the conditions for others while contributing to our own wellbeing. We all struggle with the human condition from time to time, and doing what we can to lighten the load for each other is fundamental to our mutual thriving.

The bottom line:

The way to become more skilled at presence, purpose, cultivation, and connection is to practice them. If you do not want to be more skilled at these things, then do not practice them – that's how it works.

Mindful Self-Regulation

*Tell me, what is it you plan to do with
your one wild and precious life?*
~ Mary Oliver

Andy woke up most mornings with a sense of
anxiety about the day ahead or some stress about
something that happened the day before. He
would check his email on his phone first thing,
and generally find more to worry about. As he
showered and got dressed, he would spend his
time mentally searching for the cause of his
anxious feelings. He described it as feeling like
there was an animal strapped to his chest that he
was feeding. He would try to distract himself from
the discomfort with some entertainment, some
busywork, or some food. He went to bed at night
to the soundtrack of an internal monologue about
the problems that needed his attention the next
day. He hoped for the day when these thoughts
and feelings would go away. With practice, he
discovered that while he may not be able to keep
these thoughts and feelings from showing up, he
did not have to feed them either. In the absence of
reinforcement, they began to show up with less
frequency and intensity.

We can lighten up and focus. Mindful self-regulation begins with bringing awareness and acceptance to circumstances as they are so that we can focus attention and energy on what is most important and effective. It is the practice of working peacefully with whatever shows up, cultivating powerful internal resources, and choosing a purposeful response based on what matters most.

We can notice thoughts and feelings and let them pass. This may not seem like a big deal, but it is a very big deal. In the absence of conscious awareness our behavior is driven by sensations. Some of these sensations are experienced as physical urges and impulses, while other sensations are experienced mentally as thoughts. The ability to observe sensations and to make a conscious choice about whether to engage in the behavior that is associated with them – that is nothing short of a superpower in the animal kingdom.

We may only have free won't. It is possible that free will is a figment of the human imagination. It may be that the best we can do is veto an action that is inspired by a sensation.

Try this. Set a timer for two minutes. Bring your attention to the sensations of your breath and keep it there for the full two minutes. It is likely that almost immediately your mind will wander, you will get distracted, or some tension, boredom, or worry will show up. You may feel pleasant sensations or you may feel discomfort. The beginning of mindful self-regulation is simply noticing and accepting any and all of this as normal human experience.

To be human is to have a whole range of experience. Fear, anger, anxiety, stress, sadness, frustration, resentment, restlessness, and boredom are all normal. Some of the most beautiful and inspiring experiences in life are the result of challenge, difficulty, and discomfort.

You can learn to be with all of it. How we relate to our emotions has a huge impact on the quality of our lives – we tend to cling to some and push others away. This takes a fair amount of energy. Simply being present – practicing awareness and acceptance – can be a game changer.

The benefits of mindful self-regulation include:

More consistent focus on the goals, commitments, and relationships that you value most deeply

More graceful and effective responses to stress, anxiety, distraction, and setback

Easier access to positive internal resources that support a more peaceful life

Stronger relationships with others through clear, kind, and assertive communication and action

This approach is research-based and time-tested. This practice is based on principles derived from the study of neuroscience, human development, and behavioral psychology. It is also informed by lasting wisdom from major contemplative traditions. Mindful self-regulation been practiced in different forms for thousands of years, and it is gaining more support everyday from modern science.

Shaping your brain takes practice over time. It is repeated behavior that wires your brain for a peaceful and powerful life. Breakthroughs and epiphanies are great, but they do not create lasting change on their own. Incorporating this practice into daily life is the surest path.

The bottom line:

Bringing awareness and acceptance to what is actually happening allows us to put energy into what we value most.

Mindfulness

*Mindfulness is about love and loving
life. When you cultivate this love,
it gives you clarity and compassion
for life, and your actions happen in
accordance with that.*
~ Jon Kabat-Zinn

One night, while getting ready for bed, I was
thinking about a talk on mindfulness that I was
going to give the next day. Standing in front of the
bathroom mirror, I squeezed some paste onto my
toothbrush and began to brush. A wave of greasy
bitterness flooded my mouth. Confused, I looked
down at the tube on the sink. Yup, I was brushing
my teeth with sunscreen. Another great reminder
that thinking about mindfulness and being
mindful are not the same thing.

Mindfulness is the skillful use of attention. Mindfulness includes noticing where your attention is, accepting what you find, and returning it where you choose. Anytime you are consciously bringing your attention, with acceptance, to what is going on within you or around you, you are being mindful.

Attention wanders. Getting distracted is normal. With practice, you can notice sooner and sooner when your attention has wandered, and you can make the choice to bring it back to what is happening in the present. Mindfulness practice is a great metaphor for life – we focus, we get distracted, we notice that we are distracted, and we bring our focus back. That's all.

Mindfulness is the practice of paying attention to our experience with honest, compassionate acceptance. Because you are human, you feel a lot of different things. Some of these are pleasant and some are not. Some feelings are useful guides for your behavior and some are not. Setting aside time to notice and accept this reality of being human strengthens the clarity and freedom you need to work skillfully with the full range of human emotions.

Mindfulness is not the same as relaxation.
You might find that you relax when you practice,
and you might notice that you are tense or bored.
All of this is normal. The point is to bring
attention and acceptance to the way things are at
the moment. You can be mindful of restlessness,
stress, anxiety, or any other internal experience.
You can be mindful of a sound, an image, the
temperature of the air, or any other external
experience.

**Paying attention with acceptance creates
some space.** When you step back and observe
thoughts and sensations, it allows you to see that
they are only thoughts and sensations. Rather
than counting solely on passing feelings, a bit of
distance allows you to include enduring values
and commitments in the mix when making
choices.

**Working with what is going on inside you
is the foundation.** If you can work peacefully
and powerfully with anything going on inside you,
then you can work peacefully and powerfully with
anything going on around you. Mindfulness helps
you work skillfully with a range of emotions,
which in turn, helps you self-regulate your

behavior. When you are mindful, you can look at your current conditioning – your perceptions, thoughts, feelings, and beliefs – with fresh and friendly eyes.

You can be honest and kind with yourself. Rather than putting energy into avoiding discomfort or judging yourself harshly, you can practice being aware and accepting of what is happening, what is working, and what is not working. This clarity becomes the foundation for choosing and adopting more effective behavior. You can bring a bit of humor and humility to the challenges you face. You can lighten up just a bit.

The bottom line:
We can learn to use our attention quite skillfully – it just takes practice.

Ask yourself

If you were more mindful, how would it help you work more skillfully with life?

Self-Regulation

Neurocircuitry may be neurocircuitry,
but we don't have to
run on automatic.
~ Jill Bolte Taylor

Donuts, cheesecake, maple syrup on pancakes, candy bars – Donna loved it all. The thing is, she often felt terrible after eating refined sugar. Despite this, she felt the urge to say yes whenever something sweet was offered. When she went shopping, she would end up bringing home food that she wished she hadn't. If her cravings were the only information she used to make her decisions about sugar, then she would always say yes. Always. She worked on experiencing that there is always a choice – even in the face of powerful desire. Rather than continue to wish for the day that cravings would not show up, she practiced accepting the presence of cravings and making a conscious choice based on longer-term health. This became a powerful source of confidence and freedom for Donna.

Let's be honest, sometimes you feel like doing what is important and sometimes you do not. All things being equal, I would rather not pay my taxes. My preference would be to keep my money and spend it on the things I like. And, the choice to not pay my taxes does not line up with my long-term goal of staying out of jail.

Self-regulation is the skillful use of attention and energy. Human beings have an amazing ability to align our behavior with our highest goals and deepest values, even when we don't feel like it. This amazing human ability – self-regulation – is at the heart of a good life. Self-regulation can be broken down further into self-discipline and self-control. Self-discipline is the ability to say yes when you feel like saying no and self-control is the ability to say no when you feel like saying yes.

Self-regulation includes training, cultivation, and response. You can train in skills you would like to strengthen – such as listening to others or playing the guitar. You can cultivate internal resources such as awareness, acceptance, gratitude, compassion, and awe. You can exercise the choice of how you respond to what is happening. Spending time and energy training, cultivating, and responding based on values has a positive, compounding effect on the quality of your life.

Self-regulation is a key to spontaneity. Self-regulation can sound pretty sterile and rigid, however, without this skill, you are a slave to every passing thought and feeling. Self-regulation allows you to compare what you are feeling and thinking to what is deeply important. Choosing behavior on purpose, and accepting responsibility for those choices, are incredible sources of authentic confidence and freedom.

Sometimes the only way to discover what works is by experimenting. Sometimes you don't feel like you have a choice to do things differently. Sometimes doing something new comes with fear or other forms of resistance. Sometimes it takes a leap of faith to run an experiment. The power of self-regulation allows you to explore new possibilities in the face of conditioned resistance.

The bottom line:

*Putting your energy into what you value most –
especially when you don't feel like it – is an
incredible source of power and authentic
confidence.*

Ask yourself

What is one area of your life where it would benefit you to more closely align your values and your behavior?

Your Brain

We see the world not as it is,
but as we are.
~ Anais Nin

Esref Armegan was born without eyes. He has never "seen" the world the way we think sighted people do. What does this man do for a living? He is a painter. He paints landscapes, still life, and portraits. I dare say that any sighted person looking at his work would have no reason to believe that the creator was blind. How does he "see" what he is painting? The same way you do. When you close your eyes at night and dream, where are those images coming from? Not your eyes.

Your brain is a dark place. There is no light in your there – no sound, taste, smell, or touch. Your sensory neurons translate everything happening around you into patterns of electro-chemical energy that are used by your brain to create the model of reality that you experience. It's all internally constructed.

No one sees objective reality. No one. If you believe that you see the world the way it is, then there is only one logical explanation for people who see it differently – they are wrong. However, if you keep in mind that everyone has a unique, internally created model, then you can work more skillfully with differing perspectives.

Not everything you believe is useful. There are some parts of your model of reality that work beautifully, and there are some parts that are not helpful. It can be very useful to pay attention to what your brain tells you and to test it from time to time. In doing so, you can get a better sense of whether a belief is useful or limiting.

Your Two Brains

*There is nothing either good or bad,
but thinking makes it so.*
~ William Shakespeare

Craig was a very successful young man. When we
met he was in mid thirties and retired. During one
of our conversations he appeared quite stressed,
and he told me that he would not be able to
concentrate until he made a phone call. After the
call, I asked him if everything was okay. He let me
know that he was in the middle of a deal with
eleven million dollars on the line. "So, if things go
badly, you could lose eleven million dollars?" I
asked. "No, I stand to make thirty million dollars.
If things go badly, I will only make eleven."
Craig's problem for the day was that he might
only make eleven million dollars. As extreme as
this sounds, I realized that there were many
situations in my own life that felt like problems to
me, but that others would love to have. And then I
remembered that Maggie viewed terminal cancer
as the greatest opportunity of her life. Eleven
million dollars as a problem and cancer as an
opportunity – welcome to your two human brains.

You have (at least) two brains. It can be useful to think of yourself as having two major systems in your brain. One of these systems is responsible for keeping you alive. The other system is responsible for prioritizing goals and values. We can refer to these respectively as the survival and the growth systems.

Nothing in the human nervous system is simple. The human brain may be the single most complex item in the universe. However, thinking about your brain from the perspective of survival and growth gives a framework for understanding why you do things that conflict with your values and how you can take purposeful action even when you don't feel like it.

The survival system is necessary for learning and for creating automatic behavior. The survival system is the seat of habit, and it allows you to do an amazing number of things on autopilot. At this very moment, your survival system is scanning your environment for potential threats – it is the system that tenses your body when you hear a loud noise. This system can also lead you to yell at someone you love, or stare into the refrigerator late at night despite the fact that you are not hungry.

Your survival system stores associations. Seeking patterns allows your brain to learn from past experience. It stores connections between patterns in your environment and automatic behavior. These connections allow your brain to conserve energy by engaging in preprogrammed responses. The challenge is that, in its eagerness not to miss a potential threat, this system can make false associations between some behaviors and your survival. You can be left with habits that aren't useful or, in some cases, even destructive.

The growth system is necessary for prioritizing commitments and organizing time. This system is capable of incorporating information beyond what feels familiar and comfortable. This means that you have the incredible ability to do something even when you do not feel like it in the moment. You also have the ability to refrain from a behavior even when you feel like doing it.

You need both systems. Being able to store repetitive behaviors and control them unconsciously is really helpful – so is being able to consciously override urges that lead to unproductive behavior. One of the most incredible things about being human is that you can consciously use your growth system to install or uninstall automatic behaviors within the survival system through consistent, deliberate practice.

It takes energy to consciously choose behavior. This is why engaging in a new behavior or changing old habits can feel uncomfortable. When we engage in an old habit, our survival system creates comfort or reward. Many of the unpleasant sensations we experience when we try something new are there to drive us back to habitual behavior. This means that the acceptance of discomfort is a necessary part of change.

The bottom line:
The goal of mindful self-regulation is getting the survival system and the growth system in your brain to work together more of the time.

Ask yourself

How would life be different if you kept in mind that your view of reality is just one possible way of seeing things?

How do the survival and growth systems in your brain show up in your life?

Events and Stories

We are disturbed not by things, but by the view which we take of them.
~ Epictetus

Sometimes my wife asks me "have you fed the dogs?" Immediately, my brain tells me is that she is frustrated that I am not doing more around the house. So, I sputter something about how busy I am, and how sorry I am, and how I will be better in the future... Here's the thing – she just wants to know if the dogs have eaten.

The human brain is a storyteller. One of the greatest abilities of our species is the capacity to tell stories. This leads to great literature, music, poetry, art, and communities of shared purpose. Culture is passed from one person to another and across time using stories that give meaning. Some of our stories are useful or inspiring and some of our stories are limiting and oppressive. This is the nature of stories.

Stories just show up. Your brain instantly assigns meaning to stuff. If you said good morning to someone and they did not respond, that would be an event. The story is whatever you think that this event means about you, the other person, and the world. Our stories are based on our past conditioning. They feel like the truth and they affect how we behave.

You experience your stories as thoughts and sensations. Bringing awareness to these stories allows you to see them for what they are – the result of activity in your nervous system. They have no mass and no volume. They have no solid form whatsoever.

We confuse stories and events. Once meaning has been assigned to something, it can feel inseparable from the thing itself. If we are not aware of the difference between what happens and what we think it means, then we respond to our stories about the event rather than the event itself. We may not see the difference between "he is a jerk" and "my story is that he is a jerk." We may not see the difference between "something is wrong with me" and "my story is that something is wrong with me." We can get so attached to our stories that we retell some of them over and over for decades, even though we feel terrible each time we do.

We can distinguish between stories and events. One of the quickest ways to put upset in perspective is to see the distinction between what is happening and what you think it means. You can look at your stories with curiosity and see if there is any actual evidence to support them.

If your story leads to struggle, you are free to let it drop. You are free to choose a response to any event based on what is most important and within your control. You can even let go of stories that you have been holding onto for a lifetime. The ability to separate stories and events creates the freedom to use anything that shows up as an opportunity to put your energy into what is most important. With practice, all of this can happen in the time it takes to breathe a single breath.

A sense of humor helps. When you accept that these stories (made of nothing more than thoughts and sensations) are just going to keep showing up no matter what you do, you can develop a sense of humor about them. You can reclaim the energy that used to go into the avoidance, resistance, or indulgence of passing thoughts and sensations. You can transform obstacles into opportunities, frustration into insight, and struggle into freedom.

The bottom line:

Events and the stories we tell about them are not the same thing. We can find some freedom in seeing the difference.

Ask yourself

What is one story about
yourself, the world, or someone
else that you have been holding
onto even though it isn't working?

If you recognized it as a story,
(and maybe even let go of it)
what freedom or possibility
would that create in your life?

Effort and Struggle

In struggling against anguish one never produces serenity; the struggle against anguish only produces new forms of anguish
~ *Simone Weil*

Have you ever had something happen at the perfectly wrong time? Your car won't start, the ATM is out of order, your child throws up, you find a major typo on the document you just sent out... All that is needed in these moments is a new plan or a pivot of focus. However, it is easy to spend a tremendous amount of energy ruminating about how completely unfair this turn of events is. Each of us has places in our lives where we can pivot quickly, and each of us has places where we get stuck in an internal spiral about how things should have been different. This is not because there is something wrong with us; it is because we are human.

Living requires effort. There is a certain amount of energy that is necessary to live a life. Some things are physically difficult – running, lifting heavy things, jumping, climbing stairs – they demand a lot of energy. We also burn calories planning, choosing, and executing mental tasks of all kinds throughout the day. Effort is the energy required to do stuff.

Struggle is extra. The energy we put into resisting or clinging to the ways things are, trying to manage what is outside our control, or habitually engaging in ineffective behaviors – this is struggle. Putting energy into struggle can lead to exhaustion, frustration, overwhelm, isolation, and even illness.

We struggle because we are conditioned to do so. The survival system in your brain sees the world through the lens of problems, obstacles, and threats. This system is necessary to live a life, but it can create struggle where none is necessary. It can also be convincing in its insistence that you have no choice but to struggle.

"This is hard." When you imagine having a difficult conversation with a friend or relative, you may feel some discomfort. The translation of this discomfort is often "this is hard." So we put off the conversation. In fact, having the conversation may only burn a few calories, but the resenting, dreading, and avoiding the conversation can consume quite a bit of energy.

Changing behavior often fits in the category of "hard." When you think about doing something differently or starting a new practice, you may run into the thought "this is hard." It is worth asking, "is this really difficult, or is it just associated with some discomfort?" When you are aware and accepting of your conditioning, you can see the difference between effort and struggle. You can put your energy into working with life rather than against it.

The bottom line:

A lot of our energy in life is lost to struggle. We can reclaim much of this energy and put it into the effort of living a rich and meaningful life.

Ask yourself

What is a situation in your life
where you add unnecessary
struggle?

How would things be different if
you only put the necessary
effort into the situation?

Discomfort

Faith includes noticing the mess, the emptiness and discomfort, and letting it be there until some light returns.
~ Anne Lamott

My oldest son plays soccer in college. In his second year, he tore a ligament in his knee. Everyone in our family was upset. He was in a lot of pain – emotional and physical. And he got through it. We all did. It did not feel great much of the time, but everyone survived. In fact, there was something empowering about having something happen that we had all been afraid of, and getting through it. There is no way around this simple fact – the potential cost for doing something that we love is the discomfort that comes with setback and disappointment. This is life – if we are going to play, then it is likely we will get hurt. And it is just as likely that we will get through it.

Discomfort is normal. Being human includes a full range of feelings – some pleasant and some unpleasant. Even though many of us were taught from a young age that discomfort is something to be avoided, it is a normal part of being human.

Discomfort points to values. When you are feeling upset, it is often because you feel that something you value is at risk. You can use discomfort as a reminder of what is important to you. In order to gain insight from discomfort, it is helpful to realize your capacity to experience it without resistance, resentment, or resignation.

Freedom from discomfort does not require its absence. Freedom comes from the ability to consciously choose a response to discomfort based upon your lasting values. You can find freedom in the presence of discomfort rather holding out hope that you can arrange your life so that discomfort ceases to shows up.

No one dies of discomfort. But plenty of people die trying to avoid discomfort. People become addicted to substances, go deeply in debt, lash out at others, isolate themselves, and even take their own lives in an effort to escape physical and emotional pain.

Your relationship to discomfort may be the most important relationship in your life. You can learn to "be with" discomfort. You do not need to go to war with, or be a slave to how you are feeling. You can observe what is going on inside you with a peaceful stance and choose a purposeful response.

Growth requires practice. Practice includes failure. Failure is not a detour; failure is baked into any worthwhile endeavor. Ever watch a skateboarder learn a new trick? Fail. Fail. Fail. Fail. Glimmer of progress. Fail. Fail. Fail. Glimmer of progress. Failure is simply not getting the result you wanted. That's all. If you do not want to fail, then don't try.

Failure includes discomfort. It is easy to talk about failure in the abstract, but I have not found the person who likes the feelings that come with failure. We can acknowledge the discomfort that comes with failure without letting it drive us away from what matters to us.

Working mindfully with discomfort builds authentic self-confidence. The practice of facing discomfort consciously and choosing a response based on what is most important gives you evidence that you are capable of facing whatever shows up in life.

The bottom line:

Rather than putting your energy into avoiding discomfort, you can focus on growth, learning, contribution, and connection.

Ask yourself

How do you avoid discomfort?

What are some unintended side effects of this avoidance?

How would your life be different if you accepted this discomfort and did not put energy into avoiding it?

Anxiety

*You gain strength, courage, and
confidence by every experience
in which you really stop
to look fear in the face.*
~ Eleanor Roosevelt

At one point in my life, I was so overwhelmed
with anxiety that I would lie in a fetal position in
the middle of my living room floor. I wanted to be
rid of the experience more than anything. A friend
suggested that I could accept the experience,
learn from it, and work with it positively. That was
one of the only times in my life that I seriously
thought about killing another person.* Despite my
initial reaction, I did reach a point where I gave up
on getting rid of my anxiety. I found that I could
have a peaceful relationship to it. Ironically, I am
now actually grateful to have anxiety in my life –
it is such a visceral reminder to practice. Decades
later, I can see my friend's wisdom.

*Just for the record, I did not act on this impulse.

Anxiety is a real physiological experience. It involves systems of the body designed to keep you safe in the presence of a real physical threat. Anxiety can be activated with a thought or belief. This means that your body can get completely geared up in the absence of an actual threat.

The opposite of anxiety is faith. One of the primary beliefs that can hold anxiety in place is that you know what the future is going to bring and that you are not going to be able to deal with it. Faith, on the other hand, is the belief that you don't know what is going to happen in the future and that you have what you need to deal with whatever shows up. You have a tremendous amount of evidence from your life that this is true – unexpected and unwanted things have happened many times, and you have always dealt with them.

Acceptance is a powerful way to work with anxiety. Because anxiety is so uncomfortable, it is understandable that you want to get rid of it when it shows up. Ironically, this can actually intensify the experience. When you treat anxiety as a threat, you engage the same part of the nervous system that created it in the first place. As bizarre as it may sound, acceptance of anxiety often allows you to work with it more effectively.

Acceptance is not the same as resignation. Resignation is based on the notion that nothing can be done. Acceptance is simply the acknowledgment that what is happening is happening. You can bring awareness and acceptance to the actual physical experience – tightness of the chest, throat, or stomach, increased heart rate and breathing, racing thoughts, etc…

Confidence is a relationship to uncertainty. One of the ways that people comfort each other is to say things like "everything is going to work out just fine." This is a well-intentioned thing to do, but in reality, no one knows what is going to happen in the future. Convincing yourself that things will work out the way you want them to can lead to a fragile confidence that is dependent on circumstances that are largely outside your control.

Authentic confidence comes from the acceptance of uncertainty about future events combined with the experiential knowledge that you can work with whatever shows up. Of course, there may be discomfort that comes with challenge, but the fact that you are reading this is evidence that you have always survived discomfort.

The bottom line:

Anxiety is real. You can fuel it through resistance or you can accept it and let it pass while you put your energy into living your life.

Ask yourself

How would life be different for you if you felt in your gut that you always have the internal resources you need to deal with whatever happens?

Compassion

Vulnerability is the birthplace of connection and the path to the feeling of worthiness.
~ Brene Brown

Have you ever stood in an airport, a coffee shop, or at the grocery store and just watched the people with all your heart? Have you ever stopped to feel the humanity around you – the hopes, dreams, struggles, and heartbreak? If you take the time to really look and feel, you may see that all human beings are doing the best they know how – even the ones who drive you crazy. You may feel the weight that each of us carries as we worry about what is going to happen and whether we are up to it. You may realize that in the face of human struggle, compassion is the only thing that makes sense.

Perfection is not the goal. A spirit of compassion is fundamental to mindful self-regulation. Judgment and blame are not necessary in order to focus your attention and energy on what is most important or to learn from the moments when you don't. Anything can become a vehicle for perfectionism, so it is worth watching out for how it shows up in your practice.

Judgment is natural and normal – fueling it is not part of this practice. Without self-acceptance and self-compassion, this practice can easily become a vehicle for harsh self-judgment. And without acceptance and compassion for others, mindful self-regulation can be used to feed self-involvement and egotism.

Much of the anxiety and stress we face comes from how hard we are on ourselves. It is easy to get caught in the illusion that there is a razor thin path of success or a definition of "doing it right." On either side of this knife's edge we imagine a drop into a life of rejection, isolation, and flavorless mediocrity.

There are voices in our heads. Many of us travel through the world with voices in our heads that are constantly reminding us of how we are falling short. These voices are so familiar that we fail to see it as anything other than the truth.

Treating our critical voices like the truth has a cost. We end up defending ourselves from ourselves and endlessly trying to prove ourselves to ourselves. Sometimes the voice can feel so relentless that we just give up trying altogether. Compassion is the practice of letting down our guard and vulnerably acknowledging that we are human — that we are no more or less miraculous than anyone else. The enduring wisdom of "Love thy neighbor as thyself" suggests that each of us is as deserving of our love and kindness as anyone else.

Self-compassion supports courage. There is deep psychological safety that comes from accessing self-compassion. From this place of safety, we can listen to viewpoints that differ from our own, we can reach out with kindness to people even when we don't know how they will respond. We can take risks in the name of our values, even when our choices may not be popular. We can free ourselves from the dependence on the validation of others, and we can release the need to criticize others in order to elevate ourselves.

Compassion allows us to be curious about other ways of seeing the world. Rather than rigidly defending our view as if we were defending our physical selves, we can accept that there are many ways to see the world. Compassion also allows us to stand up for ourselves and be assertive about what we want in the face of uncertainty about the reaction we will get.

The bottom line:

Being human contains discomfort and struggle. We can meet this reality with an open heart, and simply support each other and ourselves.

Ask yourself

How would your life be different
if you had greater compassion
for others?

How would your life be different
if you had greater compassion
for yourself?

Rest, Move, Fuel

Take care of your body.
It's the only place you have to live.
~ Jim Rohn

Anthony worked incredibly hard. He never missed a deadline and always kept his commitments. He slept as much as his schedule allowed – usually between four and six hours a night. For years, he had been promising himself that he would begin exercising, but he could not seem to find time on his calendar. When he did take time for lunch, it was almost always fast food on the run. He had been able to cope for years, but now his body and mind were rebelling. He was exhausted, depressed, and negative much of the time. His family found it harder and harder to be with him. Anthony was feeling pretty hopeless. He agreed to make three small changes – he established a consistent bedtime, he added a fifteen-minute brisk walk to his morning, and he packed some healthy, whole food for lunch. A month later he could not believe how much his outlook on life had changed.

Your body and your mind are inseparable.
How you experience the world has a lot to do
with how your body is functioning. The systems
of your body – nervous, immune, endocrine,
cardiovascular, digestive – are constantly working
with each other. Giving your body the sleep,
exercise, and food that it needs is a foundation for
wellbeing.

**Taking care of yourself in this way is
good for you and good for those around
you.** Your interactions and relationships with
others benefit from having a healthy body and
mind. In fact, one of the most selfless things you
can do for others is take care of yourself.

Sleep matters. It is difficult to overstate the
importance of adequate and consistent sleep.
There are many processes related to learning,
growth, and repair that only occur when we are
sleeping. Inadequate sleep is associated with
immune system function, mood, resilience to
stress, long-term memory, attentional focus,
depression, and cardiovascular health. Many
chronic health challenges diminish when we
prioritize sleep.

Movement can change your life. The human body was designed to move. There is a powerful connection between body movement and healthy brain function. In addition to cardiovascular and immune system function, consistent movement also positively affects learning, mood, and longevity. Exercise is great, but being active throughout the day is just as important. In fact, getting out of your chair, taking the stairs, and taking frequent short walks can make a big difference in the quality of your life.

A healthy gut supports a healthy brain. Food is powerful. The chemicals you put in your body, and the condition of your digestive system, have an enormous effect on your overall wellbeing. What you eat affects the trillions of bacteria in your gut, and these bacteria have a significant impact on your emotions, your cognition, and your immune system. Maximize fresh, colorful, and whole food. Minimize sweeteners (sugar and artificial) and processed foods.

The bottom line:
Good life practice uses the mind, heart and body. Taking care of your body is foundational to a good life.

Ask yourself

What are some small, consistent things you could be doing to support the health of your body?

Start Now

Whatever is happening is
the path to enlightenment.
~ Pema Chodron

Not too long ago I went to the emergency room with a nasty cough. After some initial tests, I was admitted to the hospital. I ended up spending a week in an isolation room while doctors determined that I had a rare form of leukemia. What followed were lots and lots of needles, three bone marrow biopsies, two rounds of chemotherapy, fatigue and nausea.* Despite all of this, I can honestly say that this experience was one of the best of my adult life. It gave me an amazing opportunity to practice working with physical and emotional discomfort. It also crystallized my focus on what mattered most to me – being a father to my two boys. I would never have voluntarily chosen this experience for myself, but I am so grateful to have had it.

*Treatment went well, and I am in remission.

Any circumstance offers a chance to practice. You can use a challenging relationship, a feeling of being stuck, a difficult work situation, an unwanted diagnosis, a change in your career, a financial turn, or a heartbreaking loss. You can also use a sunny day, the birth of a child, a family vacation, or a promotion at work.

The two best times to practice are when you are stressed and when you are not. When you are upset, it can be easy to lose sight of what is most important. When you are relaxed and life is going smoothly, it can be easy to lose sight of what is most important. This is why both of these times are good times to be present, purposeful, positive, and connected.

With practice, you will become more skilled at:

Noticing where your mind habitually goes

Letting go of sticky thoughts and feelings

Returning your attention to what is actually happening within you and around you

Identifying what is most important and choosing to put your attention and energy there

Having faith that you have what you need to work with whatever shows up

Being grateful and being in awe of the miracle of life

Extending kindness to yourself and others

Taking complete responsibility *for your choices.*

The bottom line:
There is never a better time to practice a good life than right now – no matter what is happening.

Planning Your Practice

Pride makes us artificial
and humility makes us real.
~ Thomas Merton

Oliver wanted to be more present and more kind
to his family when he got home from work. He
wanted to let go of whatever happened during the
day and bring his full attention to the people he
loved. Despite his best intentions, he would
regularly forget his commitment and be short with
his spouse and kids. Each time he lost his temper,
he would get down on himself and wrestle with
feelings of failure. This pattern repeated itself for
weeks, but he was still reluctant to put reminders
in his life because he felt he should be able to do
it without them. Finally, he put a sticky note on
his steering wheel so that he could look at it
before he entered his house at the end of the day.
It had two words written on it: "Be Kind." That
little piece of paper changed his life.

Reminders work. Putting simple reminders in your life can make a big difference. The survival system in your brain can easily lead you to believe that reminders are not necessary – do not fall for this. Sticky notes on your mirror, dashboard, desktop, or doorway can be very helpful. Scheduling practice on your calendar, putting reminders on your phone, or writing notes on the top of your to-do list can all be effective.

You can always begin again. The more deliberate and consistent you are, the more effective your practice will be. If you find that you forget or lose interest, that is not a problem – in fact, it is to be expected. When this happens, you can simply begin again.

Here is a beginning practice plan. The instructions for each practice (plus several more) are in the following pages. I suggest trying the first four for 30 days in a row and seeing what happens.

Mindfulness Meditation: 5 minutes a day*

Box Breathing: 4 to 6 rounds, 3 times a day

Open, Breathe, Smile: 3 times a day (or more!)

Self-compassion: 2 minutes a day

Cold Shower: 7 days in a row

The bottom line:

There is insight that comes from the commitment to practicing something and then seeing how it goes. Putting practice reminders in your life is really helpful.

*When this practice happens is not as important as doing these practices at the same time everyday. The goal is to practice whether you feel like it or not – not when you feel like it.

Ask yourself

How do you usually remind
yourself to do something?

How will you remember to
practice when you don't
feel like it?

PART TWO:
GOOD LIFE PRACTICES

*In theory, there is no difference
between theory and practice.
But, in practice, there is.*
~ Anonymous

It's All Love

*Let the beauty we love
be what we do.*
~ Rumi

My wife, Marnie, brought the phrase "It's all love" into our marriage. Sometimes we use it jokingly – like when one of our dogs chewed a favorite pair of my shoes. Sometimes we say it seriously – like when we are worried about one of our children. We use this phrase to support each other and remind ourselves how precious life is even when we are annoyed, disappointed, or anxious.

I began a practice of stopping and saying it to myself several times during the day. (I have a timer app on my phone and a watch that vibrates on my wrist as a reminder. This is the only reminder I have on my watch.) I practice by bringing my attention to my feet on the ground, taking two or three deep breaths, and smiling gently. I wait until I can feel a sense of appreciation, gratitude, and kindness in my body. The practice is more than saying the phrase to myself – it is important to feel it as well. The practice is to connect to the internal experience of love that is available at all times.

Some time ago, I was driving to a meeting at a company I was hoping to work with. I had my morning cup of coffee next to me. Someone stepped off the curb to cross the street in front of me, and I stepped on the brakes to stop quickly. My coffee went everywhere. It was as if a little tiny caffeinated volcano erupted onto the dashboard, my pants, my shirt, and all over the floor of the car.

My whole body instantly tightened, and I could feel my nervous system searching for someone to blame. And then, clear as a bell, I could hear a kind voice in my head – "it's all love." It wasn't something I consciously said to myself – all that practice had led to a helpful reminder when I most needed it.

I pulled over, cleaned up the spill, and went on my way to my appointment. I still had a big coffee stain on my pants, but this moment was the highlight of my day.

Rather than clinging to the hope that things will be the way we want then to be, we can develop the faith that no matter what shows up, we have the internal resources we need to deal with it.

As human beings we always have the choice of trying to manipulate the world around us to trigger the love that we seek. We also have the choice of cultivating love internally – independent of our circumstances. And who knows — it may show up just when we need it.

PRESENCE:
Being with what is

*The ability to be in the present
moment is a major component
of mental wellness.*
~ Abraham Maslow

What is the big deal with being present? For
starters, the present is the only time when
anything happens. The future and the past are
concepts that do not exist in any real way. Life, in
all it's complicated, miraculous glory, is
happening all around us all the time. And yet, we
humans can spend a lot of time with our attention
"somewhen" else. Practicing presence allows us
to live the one life we have a bit more fully.

Mindfulness Meditation

The faculty of voluntarily bringing back a wandering attention, over and over again, is the very root of judgment, character, and will.
~ William James

Mindfulness begins with a commitment. You simply choose something to pay attention to. It is common practice to start with the sensations of the breath, but you can use the sensations of walking, eating, or just about anything else. You can also use an object or a sound. The reason the breath can be so useful is that you always have it with you.

There is no instruction to suppress or avoid thinking. If you notice that your attention has wandered to a thought or another sensation, accept this and return your attention to the breath. There is no instruction to keep your mind from wandering. When you notice that it has wandered, just bring it back kindly and gently.

Practice:
Commit, Notice, Accept, Return

Set a timer for five minutes. Find the sensations of breathing in your body – you might notice it in the movement of your belly, the movement of your chest, or in the movement of air in your nostrils or in the back of your throat. Just notice and accept whatever happens. When you notice that your attention is someplace other than the breath, just bring it back kindly and gently.

If you notice an uncomfortable sensation in the body such as pain, anger, fear, sadness, anxiety, or stress – just bring as much acceptance as you can to that sensation and return your attention back to the breath. Sometimes it can be useful to count your breaths – "one" on the in-breath, "two" on the out-breath, and so on, up to a count of ten. When you reach ten, or if you lose count (completely normal), then simply begin again at "one."

Of course, you can also bring attention to your breath throughout each day as a way to refocus on what is happening in the present.

Breathing

Every breath we take, every step we make, can be filled with peace, joy and serenity.
~ Thich Nhat Hanh

How you breathe affects your wellbeing. One of the most effective ways you can self-regulate is with your breathing. By paying attention and breathing more slowly into a relaxed belly, you can lower levels of stress hormones in your blood stream and reduce activity in the more reactive and self-defensive parts of your nervous system. This practice builds the skill of being alert and responsive without being vigilant and reactive.

If you wait until you are stressed or anxious, it is tough to get in enough practice, and it can feel like you are using the breathing to avoid or suppress difficult feelings. Therefore, it is helpful to practice breathing throughout the day, whether you are stressed or not.

Practice:
Box Breathing

This practice is called box breathing because it takes the shape of four steps that each takes a count of four.

Begin with an in-breath for a slow count of four. As you breathe in, allow your belly to relax and fall away from your body as it fills.*

Wait gently for a slow count of four. The point of this is not to add tension, but to pause in a relaxed state.

Breathe out for a slow count of four and bring your belly button back toward your spine.

Wait gently for a slow count of four.

Begin another round by releasing your belly and breathing in for a count of four.

*Many of us are used to lifting our chest when we breathe in, so it may feel a bit awkward to allow our belly to move out when we breathe in. With practice, this will come more and more naturally.

The Cold Shower

Pain is inevitable. Suffering is optional.
~ Haruki Murakami

A cold shower is a powerful metaphor for life. When a cold shower is running, no amount of internal debate, argument, resistance, or contraction will warm the water. You can take a cold shower tightly contracted and making funny noises, or you can take a cold shower in an open and relaxed state. Either way, it is a cold shower.

Many daily events are like a cold shower. When you have a flat tire, no amount of contraction and resistance is going to fix it. It's not as if the car senses your upset and then self-inflates the tire. When you do not like what is happening in life, you can contract, resist, yell, blame, and complain. Or you can put your hands at your side and relax. The choice is yours.

One of the main sources of human struggle is resistance to our own feelings. When you commit to doing something that is likely to trigger discomfort, you can learn a lot about effort, struggle, acceptance, and what you are really capable of. You can learn about your capacity to feel stuff without having to automatically indulge or resist. Exercising this skill gives you the freedom to put your energy into what matters most. A cold shower is a great way to exercise this skill.

Practice:
Taking a Cold Shower

Turn the water temperature in your shower as cold as it will go.

As you stand outside the shower, notice any resistance to getting in.

Step in with as much acceptance of the experience as you can. Breathe deeply and calmly.

Once you get in, notice any contraction and resistance. Notice the choice to remain contracted or to let go, relax, and have the experience just as it is.

The point of this practice is not to "gut it out" or "fight through it." The point is to see that you can have the experience without adding any resistance to it.

PURPOSE:
Focusing on what matters

Nothing contributes so much to tranquilize the mind as a steady purpose - a point on which the soul may fix its intellectual eye.
~ Mary Shelley

"Find your purpose." This is a common encouragement that can lead us to believe that there is some magical calling out there that we need to discover. Practicing purpose is a bit different. It is about connecting with why you are doing whatever you are doing. If you can find no purpose for what you are doing, then it may be worth looking at more closely. Over time, you can let go of the things that do not seem to have a "why" and put more of your energy into the things that do.

Most Important

He who has a why to live
can bear almost any how.
~ Friedrich Nietzsche

Values help you focus. Being able to connect quickly with what matters most is a powerful tool for refocusing your attention and energy. The goal here is to be able to *feel* what is important, not just to have it as a concept or idea.

Practice:
Identifying What Matters

Using the questions below, write for at least 10 minutes without stopping. You don't have to answer each question – instead use them as prompts to help you keep writing for the entire 10 minutes.

What do you want to be the center of your life?

What kinds of relationships do you want to have?

How do you want to experience the world?

To what are you most deeply committed?

How do you want to help others?

What do you want to achieve?

What are you grateful for?

What needs to change?

After you have finished writing, look over what you have written. Work to distill your response into 3-5 words that represent what is most important to you. As you identify these words, pay attention to how you feel.

Spend some time asking yourself why the 3-5 things above are important. If you put your time and energy into these things, what would that get for you? Why do they matter? What is beneath them? What is at the very heart of your life?

Connect a powerful memory or an image to the feeling of what is most important to you. Connect an action – such as smiling, putting your hand on your chest, or taking a deep breath – this gives you a powerful anchor that you can return to repeatedly throughout the day.

Aligning Time and Values*

A schedule defends
from chaos and whim.
~ Annie Dillard

There is freedom in restraint. Rigidly
adhering to a plan can certainly be restrictive.
However, if you do not have a plan at all, then you
are left to organize your time around how you are
feeling at any given moment.

**A plan gives structure that supports
follow through.** Avoiding commitments and
plans – "keeping things flexible" – is often a way
for the survival system of your brain to keep your
current behavior in place.

Again, the point is not to be perfect – it is
simply to move incrementally, with conscious
awareness, toward greater alignment in your life.

*Gratitude to Sara Caputo at Caputo Consulting for
helping me with this practice.
https://www.saracaputoconsulting.com/

Practice:
Values-based scheduling

At the beginning of the week, look ahead and organize your time around what matters most to you. It is helpful to think about your most meaningful priorities – health, family, work, learning, service, etc... It is useful to limit your top priorities to 4-6 categories.

Some tasks are inherently important to you and some serve other higher purposes. At the beginning of the week – Sunday evening perhaps – set aside 15-20 minutes to look ahead at the upcoming week and make sure you have scheduled in your priorities. Is there time blocked out on your schedule for family? Exercise? Sleep? If it is important to you, then find a place for it on your calendar. If you do not, then less important activities will fill the time.

Each night, take a few minutes to look at your calendar for the day ahead and transfer this information to a daily plan. In addition to a to-do list, you can include reminders about the life you want to live and the things in your life that you want to minimize and maximize.

Making Choices

Actions express priorities.
~ Mahatma Gandhi

You always have choices. A common thing that our brains tell us is that we have no choice. "I have to", "I must", "I need to", "I can't" – these are thoughts that pop up all the time. Listen to people speak and you will hear these phrases constantly.

You are always making choices. Whether you are conscious of it or not, your brain is constantly evaluating circumstances, actions, and outcomes. In general, unconscious choices tend to be driven by what will most likely lead to a familiar outcome. Your brain often prefers a safe and comfortable outcome over the possibility of a new outcome.

New choices can expand our lives. We have the freedom to take action or refrain from taking action – even when our thoughts and sensations are telling us the opposite. Even if a new choice does not work out as we hoped, we can see that we are always free to choose to do things differently.

At any given moment, you always have at least these three choices:

Spinning. You can go around and around in your head or verbally to anyone who will listen. You can restate the problem, determine who is to blame, and identify all the things that are not fair. The difference between spinning and planning is that planning has an outcome. The great thing about spinning is that it accomplishes nothing, but at least it sucks the quality out of your life.

Taking action. You can do something. You can put energy into your values, goals, commitments, and relationships. You can have the conversation you have been putting off, get started on that project, or take responsibility for that thing that went awry.

Letting go. Instead of fueling anxiety, worry, anger, fear, frustration, and resentment, you can bring your attention to sensations in your body – your feet on the ground or your breath in your body. You can bring your attention to a deeper sense of purpose.

Practice:
Choosing Consciously

When you notice that you are spinning, consciously choose whether you will continue or whether you will put your energy into taking action or letting go. If you choose to take an action that cannot be done immediately, make a specific plan for when you will do it. If you can put it on your calendar, that is even better. If you choose to put your energy into letting go, then bring your attention to the sensations of your feet on the ground and breathing in your body.

Practice:
Using the language of choice

Pay attention to the language you use to represent your choices. Notice phrases such as "I have to", "I should", "I need to," or "I can't." These are ways that your survival brain makes you feel bad and keeps you from actually committing to a new behavior.

Practice using language such as "I can", "I will", "I am going to" or "I choose to."

Practice:
Taking responsibility

Sometimes when we apologize, it is because we are seeking a response such as "that's okay," "I forgive you," or "I am sorry too." Rather than saying "I'm sorry," you can experiment with "I accept responsibility." You can practice taking complete responsibility without expecting anything in return.

Getting Started

When I hear somebody sigh,
'Life is hard,'
I am always tempted to ask,
'Compared to what?'
~ Sydney J. Harris

Find the feelings. If you pay careful attention to the tasks you put off or avoid, you will see that there is discomfort (however mild) associated with the task. If you pay careful attention to the habit you have been trying to break, you will see that there is mild discomfort associated with refraining from the behavior.

Do the work. Rather than putting energy into resistance, argument, or complaint, you can identify the next smallest thing that moves you in the direction you want to go. Start there.

Practice:
Anticipating Feelings

Even with a calendar and a to-do list, there is always the possibility that internal resistance will show up at the time of execution. We all experience desires to avoid some of our purposeful or routine tasks and engage in more pleasant tasks. One of the most powerful things you can do is honestly acknowledge that, when the time comes to do the planned task, you may not feel like doing it. You can have a strategy in place for how to work with these moments of resistance or lack of motivation when they show up.

Practice:
Feel the Feelings,
Then Get Started

When you get to the moment of execution and you are not feeling like doing the task, you can bring your attention to how you are feeling and acknowledging whatever it is. This is a useful time to practice "yes, and" – as in "YES I am feeling x, AND I am going to do y." Next, you can identify the smallest possible action that gets things in motion – opening the computer, picking up the phone, gathering the dirty laundry, putting on your running shoes...

Self-Evaluation

The most fundamental aggression to ourselves, the most fundamental harm we can do to ourselves, is to remain ignorant by not having the courage and the respect to look at ourselves honestly and gently.
~ Pema Chodron

Self-improvement without self-compassion is self-bullying. The self-improvement voice tells you that the person you want to be is always waiting for you on some imaginary horizon – a horizon that never seems to get any closer. This is the voice that won't let you forget that there is something wrong with you, and that you need to fix it to have the life and love you seek.

We can bring clarity to our intent and the consequences. It is easy to hide behind the intentions of our actions without looking at the consequences. An honest assessment of what is working and what is not working includes both intentions and consequences. This clarity allows us to make concrete plans for improving skills through consistent practice.

Growth does not require that you beat yourself up. There is a difference between pushing yourself and punishing yourself. Being harshly critical and unkind to yourself is not the key to improving the quality of your life or performance. While many people shy away from the idea of self-compassion for fear of "going soft," this is based in a misunderstanding.

Self-compassion is not the same as self-indulgence. Being kind to yourself does not mean that you do whatever you feel like and then give yourself a pass on the consequences. You are capable of kindly holding yourself accountable for keeping your commitments and taking full responsibility when you don't.

Without self-compassion, it is easy to get focused on what is wrong with *us as a person*. This is a red herring that leads to a cycle of self-bashing that takes attention and energy away from healthy growth. With honest, self-compassionate evaluation, we can focus on *our strategies* and pivot if our current approach isn't working.

Practice:
Compassionate Self-Evaluation

Next to your to-do list, keep lists of the things you would like to minimize and maximize in your life. At the end of each day, as you look at the list, take a moment to sit quietly and connect with the feeling of kindness you have for someone you really want to support.

Looking at the list through a lens of kindness, and an interest in growth rather than self-judgment, you can honestly evaluate using whatever scale you choose. You can use a 1-10 scale or you can indicate how many times you engaged in each thing on your lists. Over time you can see trends. If there does not appear to be progress, you can ask yourself honest questions such as "Do I really want to change this?" or "Is there something getting in my way that I am not acknowledging?"

CULTIVATION:
Practicing what you seek

You cannot have an abundant crop without cultivation.
~ Plato.

Cultivation is tricky. Accessing positive internal resources can be a very powerful way to cope and they can give us a useful perspective when we are challenged. However, we can also use positive emotions to mask or suppress uncomfortable feelings. The goal of cultivation is not to use positive internal resources to avoid discomfort, but to give us the ability to be with discomfort more peacefully.

Positivity

Positive emotions are not trivial luxuries, but instead might be critical necessities for optimal functioning.
~ Barbara Fredrickson

Positivity is a resource. Feeling good all the time is not normal. To be human is to have a range of feelings. Positive internal states are valuable resources that allow us to be with life when it is challenging.

Self-defense is a reflex. Over the course of the day, the demands you face lead can you to become increasingly stressed. Your body may reflexively tighten and close your posture to protect itself. One of the ways we can balance this tendency is by opening our posture and connecting with positive resources.

Practice:
Open, Breathe, and Smile

Sitting up or standing: **OPEN** your chest, drop your shoulders, **BREATHE** deeply, and **SMILE**. From this open and alert posture, you can do any or all of the following:

Take in your surroundings. Feel your feet on the ground. Look at the scene around you. Feel the air or the sun on your face. Listen to the sounds around you.

Marvel that you exist. The fact of your existence is nothing short of miraculous – that you can read the symbols on this page, that you can breathe, and that you can experience love, pain, and joy. Bring your attention to the inconceivable miracle of existence.

Feel gratitude. Bring to mind a person, relationship, experience, or opportunity for which you are deeply grateful and appreciative. Focus your attention on this and notice the sensations in your body.

Wish others well. Bring your attention to the notion that all human beings struggle from time to time. Regardless of our background or life circumstances, we all experience discomfort. You can send sincere wishes that all beings shall find some peace in the midst of their struggles.

Kindness

*Wherever there is a human being,
there is an opportunity for a kindness.*
~ Lucius Annaeus Seneca

Kindness is good for everyone. Modern research supports what sages have been saying for thousands of years – that acts of kindness are good for the person who is doing them, good for the person who is receiving them, and good for the people who are observing them.

The human brain has a bias toward finding what is wrong. This can lead us to miss out on the wonderful little moments of simple kindness that are happening all around us in modern life. Bringing your attention to all the ways that people are looking out for each other is a powerful a way to boost your daily happiness. And if you want to be really crazy, then you can contribute some of your own small acts of kindness to the cause.

You have a choice about where you focus your attention. If you look for the ways people are being kind, and the opportunities to do the same, then you experience the world differently – you experience more connection and less isolation. There are tiny, thoughtful acts of goodness that people do for one another all the time. If you are looking for them, they are not hard not to find at all. They are everywhere. Right under your nose and around every corner. They are so common that we can easily overlook them.

Practice:
Micro-kindness

Focus your attention on the small ways that the people around you are helping and supporting each other. This is especially powerful if you are feeling annoyed or stressed.

Look for small ways to help people throughout the day – the smaller and more frequent, the better.

Self-Compassion*

If your compassion does not include yourself, it is incomplete.
~ Jack Kornfield

Self-compassion supports a good life. Self-compassion comes from the experiential understanding that who you are – right here, right now – is whole, complete, and as deserving of your love and kindness as anyone else. A phrase many of us are familiar with is "Love thy neighbor as thyself." In practice, many of us just ignore the second half of this wisdom.

Self-compassion is not the same as letting yourself off the hook. You are actually more likely to take responsibility for your choices when you feel that it is okay to be human and that you can be kind to yourself even when you blow it.

* Gratitude to Jay Fields for helping me with this practice. http://jay-fields.com/

It is a skill to be kind to yourself. If you don't treat yourself with kindness, you may end up seeking validation from others. Without self-compassion we are more likely to become self-defensive or defeated in the face of any feedback that is not positive. In fact, when you are self-compassionate, you are more likely to accept responsibility without defensiveness, hold yourself accountable without excuses, and bounce back more quickly from disappointment.

You may fear how hard you will be on yourself if things do not go the way you want them to. However, you can practice being kind to yourself whether things go the way you want them to or not. If you feel that you will be kind to yourself no matter what, then you can step into the unknown with authentic confidence.

Resistance is normal. Because self-compassion is a new practice for many of us, there may be considerable resistance to this at first. This resistance results from the conditioned belief that you are not enough – that you are not as deserving of love and kindness as others.

Practice:
Self-Compassion

Bring to mind someone for whom you feel gratitude, fondness, and appreciation. Notice where in your body you feel the sensations of kindness toward this person. Focus your attention on the sensations and rest your hand on this area of your body. Now extend the kindness you feel for this person to yourself. (sometimes it's helpful to think of a younger you).

Or·

Stand in front of a mirror. Look yourself in your eyes with as much acceptance and kindness as possible. Wait until you can feel some kindness for the person looking back at you.

CONNECTION:
Being of service

Compassion, empathy, and humility can only arise out of recognizing that our common desires are differently expressed.
~ Robert A. Burton

There are few things more powerful in the human experience than our connection to each other. Research suggests that positive relationships may be the single greatest predictor of health, happiness, and longevity. We are biologically designed to seek belonging and to support each other. We can practice connecting with others in small ways throughout the day. We can even practice connecting with people who we don't know, don't like, or don't agree with.

.

Understanding

Everyone you meet
knows something you don't.
~ Bill Nye

Listening for understanding is a great service. If we ask and we listen, we can discover what people value. There is a reason that people talk about what they talk about – there is a value they are trying to express. Sometimes the person isn't aware themselves of what the value is until they are really listened to.

We often jump to a solution. When another human being is telling us about their experience, we often skip past understanding what they are really trying to tell us and we go into fix-it mode. Of course, there is nothing wrong with trying to help someone find a solution. However, if we don't take the time to understand, we may be trying to solve the wrong problem.

Practice:
Listening Mindfully

When another person is telling you about a situation, bring all of your attention to what they are telling you. Listen as intensely as if you were going to be tested on what you heard. When your attention wanders (which it will), you can notice this and bring it back. Listening mindfully, you may feel the physical urge to interrupt, to fix the other person, or to make the conversation about you. This is all normal. When you feel this, notice it and bring your attention back to what the other person is telling you.

Practice:
"Tell Me More"

A powerful practice for connecting with another person and refraining from taking over the conversation is simply to use the phrase "Tell me more." This is especially powerful if the person is upset or if you disagree with them. The added benefit is that it can help you listen to another person even when you have a very different perspective. This simple phrase can transform a relationship with a child, a partner, or a coworker.

Practice:
Three Questions

When you combine these questions with the practices of mindful listening and "tell me more," you can build understanding and trust in a short period of time. The questions are:

What is going on?
What feels most important right now?
How can I support you?

Asking these questions allows the other person to determine what they would like to tell you, what matters them, and how you can help. It may feel awkward at first to ask these questions, but with practice, they will feel more and more natural.

As you listen to the other person, you may notice that your attention wanders. This is normal. When this happens, you can simply return your attention to what they are saying. These questions, asked sincerely, can build a relationship from scratch or completely transform an existing relationship

Support

Disagreement is something normal.
~ Dalai Lama

Sometimes people disagree. No matter how aware, accepting, principled, kind and brilliant you are, some people are going to disagree with you and dislike you. No matter what you do, some people are going to resist and resent your efforts. And you will do the same to others.

This is no one's fault. Disagreement is a natural outcome of human biology. You can accept this and work with it, or you can resist it and be frustrated and exhausted. It can be helpful to remember that you can feel certain about your opinion without any factual evidence. It can be also be useful to keep in mind that listening, understanding and supporting do not require agreement.

We are living in a time when opposing the "other" appears to be the default. Political debate, news reporting, and social movements often feel that they are defined by what they are against rather than what they are for. Whether it is because of skin color, gender, ethnicity, country of origin, economic status, political beliefs – lines of opposition are being drawn, access is being denied, names are being called, and self-righteousness is being justified.

Perhaps more concerning is that listening, understanding, compassion, decency, and basic human connection are being confused with weakness or a lack of conviction. This is to the detriment of our physical, psychological, and social health. The courage to connect in the face of conflicting views or disparate backgrounds is one of our greatest attributes as human beings.

It is human to feel threatened or defensive when others express their disagreement. This does not mean that we do not have the capacity to listen to them and understand their viewpoint. In the presence of fear or anger, it is possible to hear someone and appreciate that they have a particular view of the world. It is possible to learn something in these situations without sacrificing our principles. When we become aware of disagreement, we can work with it even when it triggers discomfort.

We can be assertive and kind. Sometimes our strategy is to be passive rather than expressing an opinion or making a request. Sometimes our strategy is to aggressively express our opinions and demands. There is a vast space between being passive and being aggressive. In this space we can express ourselves authentically, kindly and assertively.

Disagreement offers a great opportunity to build a relationship. When someone is angry or resistant, we can actively explore their point of view. Rather than avoid them or argue with them, we can listen and consider their perspective. Assertive and kind communication allows us to find a balance between expressing honestly what we think, want, and need and listening to the thoughts, needs and wants of others.

Practice:
The Rule of Thirds

It can be helpful to assume that no matter what you do, a third of people may like you, a third may not, and a third just don't care. Rather than focusing on how others feel about you, you can focus on practicing what is most important. You are free to be as kind, supportive, and helpful as you can be and everyone else is free to feel about you however they feel about you.

Practice:
Default to Support

You can practice prioritizing connection over the need to be right. When you feel the need to argue or get your way, you can practice being supportive of others. It is helpful to notice the physical urge to correct or convince someone of your point of view – this is conditioning. In a moment, when you feel the urge to defend yourself, you can practice letting the urge pass and simply listening to the other person.*

This practice can have a profound impact on a partnering, parenting, or professional relationship. This practice does not mean you give up on your principles. If you pay attention, you will see that there are plenty of places in your life where your desire to get your way is not based on a principle – it is based on a passing feeling.

*It is important to acknowledge that abusive relationships do exist. I am not suggesting that you should stay and listen to someone if they are being abusive. However, I am suggesting that making a principled choice to take care of yourself does not require argument.

141

Practice:
"I Get It, And"

This phrase allows us to place two or more viewpoints side by side. The word "but" automatically creates conflict between two perspectives. Using the phrase *"I get it, and..."* can be a great practice for recognizing someone else's viewpoint without letting go of your own. It allows you to be both accepting and assertive rather than passive or aggressive.

Practice:
Communicating Assertively

Rather than:

Holding onto expectations internally and being disappointed or angry when others do not read our minds, or

Demanding that others do or see things the way we want them to,

We can feel the discomfort of vulnerability and practice expressing our viewpoint or asking for what we want.

Others are still free to disagree or turn down our request, but that does not change our freedom to be kind, direct, and assertive.

Beginning Again

Always we begin again
~ John McQuiston

**No matter how much you practice, you
are still human.** For the rest of your life you are
going to say and do things that just don't work.
You will have impulses and urges right up to the
moment of your death. There is no escape from
the human condition. Coming to peace with
being human does not mean that you are no
longer dealing with being human.

Not practicing is part of the practice. Any
moment when you notice that you are not
practicing is an opportunity to begin practicing
again. It does not matter if it has been minutes,
hours, days, months, or years since you practiced
last. All you need to do is begin again. Take a
breath, feel your feet on the ground, and connect
to what really matters. That's all.

About the Author

Dave grew up on a farm in Western New York where his family raised sheep and thousands of guinea pigs (seriously). He now lives in Southern California with his wife, two boys, and three dogs.

He graduated from Williams College, received a Master's in Humanistic and Multicultural Education from SUNY New Paltz, and he has completed a clinical internship in Mindfulness Based Stress Reduction (MBSR) at the University of Massachusetts Medical Center.

After teaching human development, neuroscience, leadership, and physics for more than 20 years in independent schools, Dave founded Applied Attention Coaching and Consulting.

Applied Attention gives individuals and teams the tools they need to live and work peacefully and powerfully. If you are seeking greater wellbeing, stronger relationships, more effective communication, or healthier culture, then Applied Attention may be able to help.

For coaching, training, or consulting in mindful self-regulation go to www.appliedattention.com

Resources & Further Reading

Research:

Baumeister, R. F., Heatherton, T. F., & Tice, D. M. (1994). *Losing control: How and why people fail at self-regulation.* Academic press.

Blackburn, E., & Epel, E. (2017). *The telomere effect: A revolutionary approach to living younger, healthier, longer.* Hachette UK.

Brown, B. (2015). *Daring greatly: How the courage to be vulnerable transforms the way we live, love, parent, and lead.* Penguin.

Brown, P. C., Roediger III, H. L., & McDaniel, M. A. (2014). *Make it stick.* Harvard University Press.

Burton, R. A. (2009). *On being certain: Believing you are right even when you're not.* Macmillan.

Burton, R. A. (2013). *A skeptic's guide to the mind: What neuroscience can and cannot tell us about ourselves.* Macmillan.

Chabris, C., & Simons, D. (2010). *The invisible gorilla: And other ways our intuitions deceive us.* Harmony.

Damasio, A. R. (1999). *The feeling of what happens: Body and emotion in the making of consciousness.* Harcourt.

DiSalvo, D. (2011). *What makes your brain happy and why you should do the opposite*. Prometheus Books.

Eagleman, D. (2015). *The brain: The story of you*. Canongate Books.

Eagleman, D. (2011). *Incognito: The secret lives of the brain*. Pantheon.

Emmons, R. A. (2007). *Thanks!: How the new science of gratitude can make you happier*. Houghton Mifflin Harcourt.

Fredrickson, B. (2009). *Positivity*. Harmony.

Gilbert, D. (2009). *Stumbling on happiness*. Vintage Canada.

Joseph, S. (2013). *What doesn't kill us: The new psychology of posttraumatic growth*. Basic Books.

Kahneman, D., & Egan, P. (2011). *Thinking, fast and slow* (Vol. 1). Farrar, Straus and Giroux.

Kashdan, T. (2009). *Curious? Discover the missing ingredient to a fulfilling life*. William Morrow & Co.

Kenrick, D. T., & Griskevicius, V. (2013). *The rational animal: How evolution made us smarter than we think*. Basic Books.

Kurzban, R. (2011). *Why everyone (else) is a hypocrite: Evolution and the modular mind*. Princeton University Press.

LeDoux, J. E. (2003). *Synaptic self: How our brains become who we are*. Penguin.

Lustig, R. H. (2017). *The hacking of the American mind: The science behind the corporate takeover of our bodies and brains*. Penguin.

Lyubomirsky, S. (2008). *The how of happiness: A scientific approach to getting the life you want*. Penguin.

Neff, K. (2011). *Self-compassion*. Hachette UK.

Pert, C. B. (1997). *Molecules of emotion: Why you feel the way you feel*. Simon and Schuster.

Pinker, S. (1997). *How the mind works*. Norton.

Sapolsky, R. M. (2017). *Behave: The biology of humans at our best and worst*. Penguin.

Siegel, D. J. (2010). *Mindsight: The new science of personal transformation*. Bantam.

Siegel, D. J. (2012). *Pocket guide to interpersonal neurobiology*. WW Norton & Company.

Smalley, S. L., & Winston, D. (2010). *Fully present: The science, art, and practice of mindfulness*. Da Capo Lifelong Books.

Twenge, J. M. (2017). *IGen: Why today's super-connected kids are growing up less rebellious, more tolerant, less happy--and completely unprepared for adulthood — and what that means for the rest of us*. Simon and Schuster.

Young, S. D. (2017). *Stick with it: A scientifically proven process for changing your life-for good*. HarperCollins.

Wisdom:

Aurelius, M. (2013). *Meditations*. Oxford University Press.

Brach, T. (2004). *Radical acceptance: Embracing your life with the heart of a Buddha*. Bantam.

Byron, T. (2010). *The Dhammapada: The sayings of the Buddha*. Random House.

Chödrön, P. (2010). *The wisdom of no escape: And the path of loving-kindness*. Shambhala Publications.

Covey, S. R. (1992). *The seven habits of highly effective people* (p. 358). Simon and Schuster.

Davies, O. (1994). *Meister Eckhart: Selected writings*. Penguin

Einstein, A. (2011). *Essays in humanism*. Open Road Media.

Emerson, R. W. (2012). *Self-reliance and other essays*. Courier Corporation.

Epictetus, B. (1998). *Discourses*. Clarendon Press.

Frankl, V. E. (1985). *Man's search for meaning*. Simon and Schuster.

Gandhi, M. (1983). *Autobiography: The story of my experiments with truth*. Courier Corporation.

Hanh, T. N. (2016). *The miracle of mindfulness: An introduction to the practice of meditation*. Beacon Press.

Harris, S. (2014). *Waking up: A guide to spirituality without religion*. Simon and Schuster.

Huxley, A. (2014). *The perennial philosophy*. McClelland & Stewart.

James, W. (2003). *The varieties of religious experience: A study in human nature*. Routledge.

Kornfield, J. (2009). *A path with heart: A guide through the perils and promises of spiritual life*. Bantam.

Lamont, C. (1983). *The philosophy of humanism*. Continuum

Phillips, S. (2009). *The way of a pilgrim*. Christian Spirituality: The Classics.

Rogers, C. R. (1995). *A way of being*. Houghton Mifflin Harcourt.

Rohr, R. (2017). *The way of perfection*. Whitaker House.

Seneca, S. (2016). *Letters from a Stoic*. Xist Publishing.

Thérèse, S. (1996). *Story of a soul: The autobiography of Saint Thérèse of Lisieux*. ICS Publications

Tolstoy, L., & Garnett, C. (2006). *The kingdom of God is within you*. Courier Corporation.

Valantasis, R. (2008). *The Gospel of Thomas*. Routledge.

Made in the USA
San Bernardino, CA
01 October 2018